Creative Keyboard Presents

Great Literature for Piano

BAROQUE – CLASSICAL – ROMANTIC

BOOK I
EASY

Researched and Compiled by
GAIL SMITH

Foreword

In early 19th-century Germany, the purchase of a piano commanded the interest of the new owner's entire community. The German family that ordered the piano first made a down-payment in cash. Upon completion of the piano, they paid for the balance in corn, wheat, potatoes, poultry, and firewood.

On the day that the piano was to be delivered to the new owner, the town held a festival. A band of musicians headed the procession, followed by the proud piano maker, who was borne on the shoulders of his assistants. Flowers and wreaths decorated the horse-drawn wagon which held the precious piano. Musicians, schoolmasters, and dignitaries marched in the rear.

At last the piano arrived at its destination. The delighted new owners greeted the procession warmly. The local clergyman said a prayer, blessing the new instrument as well as its craftsmen. The mayor delivered an address; the schoolmaster, doctor, and other dignitaries gave speeches. Finally, the men's chorus sang. When the piano was properly installed in its new home, everyone enjoyed a banquet and danced in celebration of this happy occasion.

In contrast, today the purchase of a piano seems no longer to be a cause for festivity and joy. Unfortunately, our generation takes such purchases for granted. We have forgotten what a treasure and gift a piano can be. We have also forgotten what a treasure and gift the great composers have given us through their beautiful musical compositions for the piano.

This new piano literature series rediscovers the "rare jewels" of piano literature. After years of research and meticulous assessment of the composers of Baroque, Classical, and Romantic music, this exciting "quest for the best" has led to a new series of eight graded books . . . all containing original compositions by the masters.

The series begins with the most easily mastered compositions, progressing to the more advanced and musically difficult selections. Pianists on all levels will enjoy this challenging, thorough, and diversified collection of piano music. In addition, an interesting biographical sketch of each composer will make these selections more meaningful to the student.

Just as flowers and wreaths decorated the horse-drawn wagon that delivered the new piano to the fortunate German villager, likewise flowers and wreaths decorate each book in this series. They serve as a reminder for us all to treasure each selection we learn and to be thankful for our magnificent musical heritage.

Gail Smith

Note to Teachers

The pieces selected in each book are in approximate order of difficulty. They are not necessarily in chronological order. Before the selections of each new composer, there is a short biographical sketch of that composer. In addition, many include a pictorial representation, as well.

Book One . . . . late primary-level and early elementary-level pieces

Book Two . . . . harder elementary pieces

Book Three . . . . medium-level or intermediate pieces

Book Four . . . . moderately difficult pieces

Book Five . . . . difficult pieces

Book Six . . . . very difficult pieces

Book Seven . . . . musically advanced sonatas

Book Eight . . . . musically advanced longer pieces

Contents
Book One

Johann Nepomuk Hummel
(November 14, 1778 – 1837)

Mozart heard Hummel play when he was very young and offered to teach him. So Hummel lived with Mozart for two years in his home at the Grosse Schulenstrasse. Hummel made his first appearance at a concert given by Mozart in 1787. Later, he studied with Clementi. Hummel became a great composer and teacher. His most famous students were Czerny and Thalberg.

Theme and Variations

Variation IV

Variation V

Variation VI

Mozart and His Family

Wolfgang Amadeus Mozart
(January 27, 1756 – December 5, 1791)

Mozart and his older sister showed amazing musical talent at a very young age. Their father, Leopold, decided to commercialize their gifts and set up concert tours in many cities, including Munich, Vienna, Paris, and London. The concerts were very successful, and the children often played for royalty. Mozart began composing at age 5 and continued writing beautiful music all his life.

Minuet

Andantino grazioso

From Leopold Mozart's Note Book

Musette

From Leopold Mozart's Note Book

Fine

12

D.C. al Fine

13

Carl Czerny
(February 20, 1791 – July 15, 1857)

Czerny's father gave him his first piano lessons. By the time he was 10, Czerny could play all the principal compositions of the best masters. Krumpholz, a family friend who knew Beethoven, took Czerny to play for him. Beethoven immediately offered to teach him. For the next three years Czerny studied with him. Czerny was always reluctant to perform in public. Instead, he spent his time composing various songs and studies that ran to "Opus 1,000." Czerny taught only pupils who showed special talent. He taught Franz Liszt.

Tonstück
(German for "a piece of music")

Carl Czerny, Op.803 No.1

Tonstück

Carl Czerny, Op.803 No. 2

Ludvig Schytte
(April 28, 1848 – November 10, 1909)

Ludvig Schytte was a great pianist and composer who was a pupil of Gade and Liszt. Schytte wrote a concerto in C♯ minor for piano, a sonata in B♭, as well as many other shorter pieces for piano.

Five Melodious Studies
Op. 108, No. 1

Etude in C
Allegro moderato (♩ = 168)

Ludvig Schytte

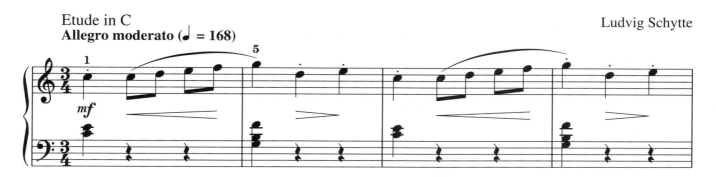

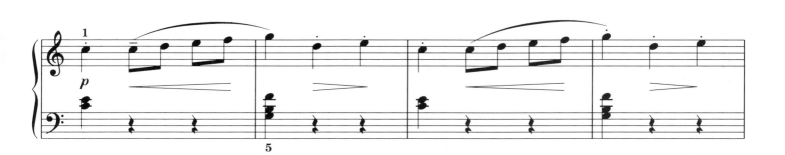

Etude in C

Op. 108, No. 2

Ludvig Schytte

Etude in E Minor

Op. 108, No. 3

Ludvig Schytte

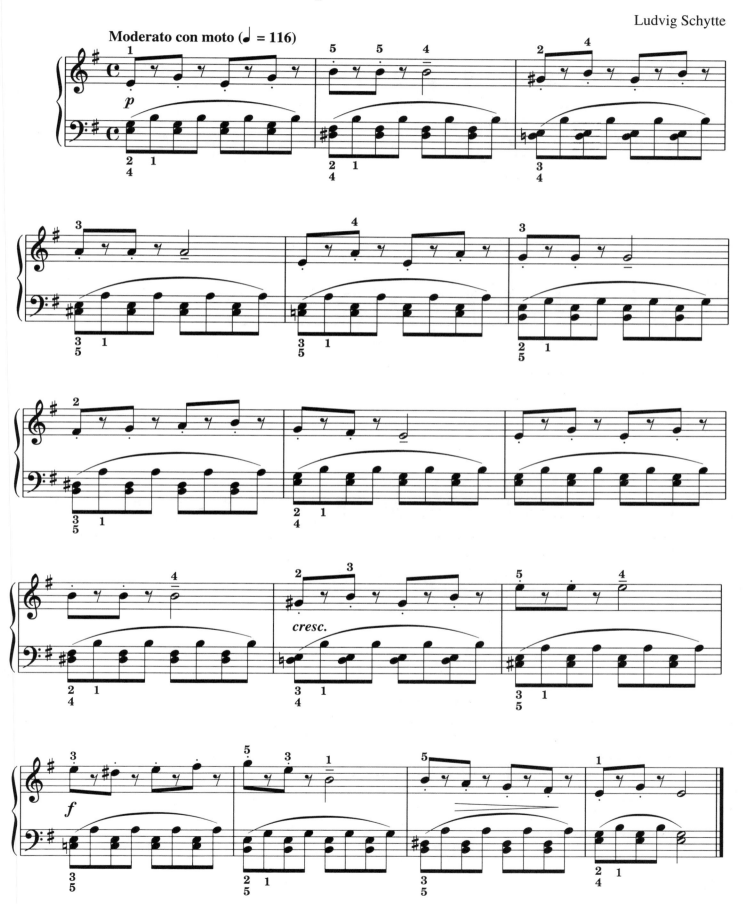

Etude in G
Op. 108, No. 12

Ludvig Schytte

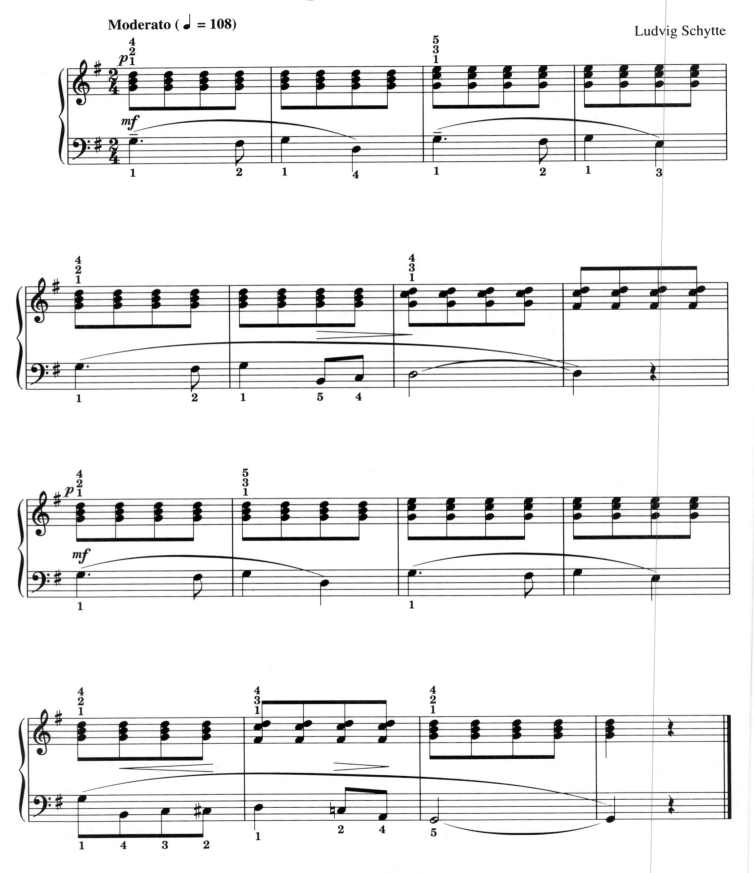

Etude in C
Op. 108, No. 13

Ludvig Schytte

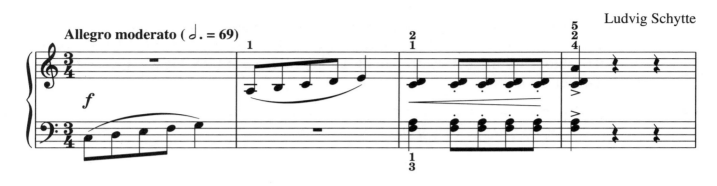

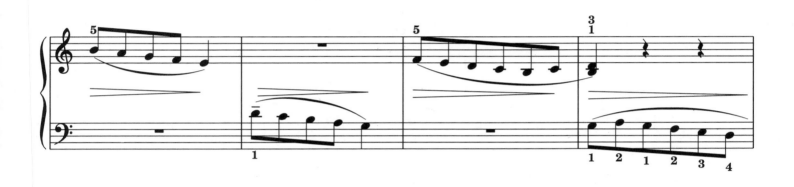

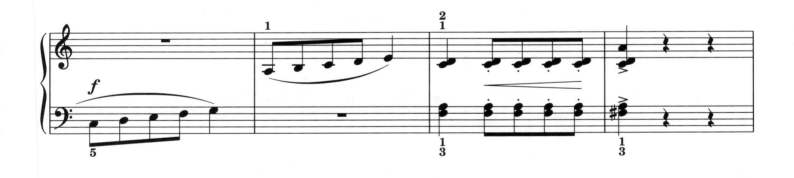

Hermann Berens
(April 7, 1826 – May 9, 1880)

Berens was a Swedish composer and pianist of German origin. He first studied music with his father, Karl Berens, a flutist and composer. He was appointed teacher of composition at the Stockholm Conservatory in 1861 and professor in 1868. He was Queen Lovisa's piano teacher for a time.

The Music Box
Op. 50, No. 17

Hermann Berens

Jean-Philippe Rameau
(September 25, 1683 – September 12, 1764)

Rameau was the son of a church organist. He became a distinguished French composer and theorist, publishing *Traite dea l' Harmonie* in 1722. In it he set forth for the very first time the law of chord inversions. Rameau used a system of chord building by thirds. His bold modulations marked an advance over his predecessors. His complete works were edited by Saint-Saens.

Rondino

Jean Philippe Rameau

Konrad Max Kunz

Kunz was a piano teacher and composer in the early 19th century. He was encouraged by Dr. Hans Von Bulow, the conductor of the Royal Court, to prepare a new edition of his *50 Canons* for piano, which had been published 30 years earlier. As Kunz worked on this project, he discarded about 30 of the original canons and ended up with a total of 200. Here are 7 of these canons.

Canon No. 22

Kunz Op.14

Canon No. 52

Kunz

Canon No. 105

Kunz

Canon No. 106

Kunz

Canon No. 126

Kunz

Canon No. 154

Kunz

Canon No. 160

Allegretto

Kunz

Song of the Sea

Cornelius Gurlitt Op.228

Theme and Variation

Andante

Gurlitt Op.228

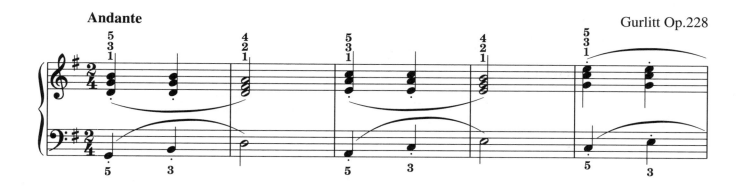

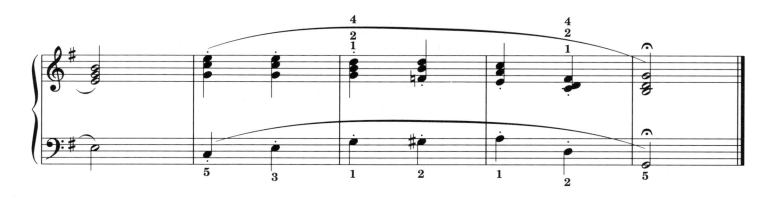

Moderato

32

Robert Alexander Schumann
(June 8, 1810 – July 1856)

To the general public, Schumann was "the husband" of Clara Wieck, concert pianist, rather than the famous composer we think of today. He wrote abundantly for the piano. He wrote numerous easier pieces for his own five children, and very difficult compositions for his wife to perform. Johann Brahms was their friend and would often baby-sit their children.

Soldiers' March
from "Album for the Young"

Robert Schumann
Op. 68, No. 2

Melody
from "Album for the Young"

Robert Schumann
Op. 68, No. 1

Jean Baptist Lully
(November 28, 1632 – March 22, 1687)

This French composer of Italian origin was the son of a miller at Florence and scarcely received any formal education. He learned his letters and how to play the guitar from a Franciscan friar. He taught himself to play the violin. From his first job working in a Paris kitchen, he ended up being instrumental composer to King Louis XIV! He married Modeleine Lambert, daughter of a court musician, in 1662, and they had three sons and three daughters. Lully died as the result of an injury to his foot, received while he was conducting a solemn "To Deum" celebrating the King's recovery from a serious illness.

Menuet in D Minor

Jean-Baptist Lully

Gigue

Samuel Arnold

Prelude

Johann Caspar F. Fischer

Ignaz Joseph Pleyel
(June 1, 1757 – November 14, 1831)

Until he was 15, Pleyel studied piano with Wanhal and then studied for five years with Haydn. He was founder of a piano factory in Paris in 1807 which prospered so quickly that he had to give his full attention to it and give up composing. At the end of his life he had written 29 symphonies, however, and much piano music.

Minuet

J.Pleyel

Trio

D.C. al Fine

44

Daniel Gottlob Turk
(1750 – 1813)

Turk was a popular German composer. He also wrote treatises on theory.

Evening Song

Daniel Gottlob Turk

The Hunters

Daniel Gottlob Turk

46

Carefree

Daniel Gottlob Turk

Rondo

Allegro

Daniel Gottlob Turk

Henri Lemoine
(October 21, 1786 – May 18, 1854)

As a child, Henri Lemoine studied at the Paris Conservatory. He became a piano teacher and wrote a piano method and many educational piano pieces. Lemoine became a music publisher, taking over the business founded by his father, Antoine Marcel.

Little Crosspatch

Allegro moderato

H. Lemoine, Op. 37, No. 24

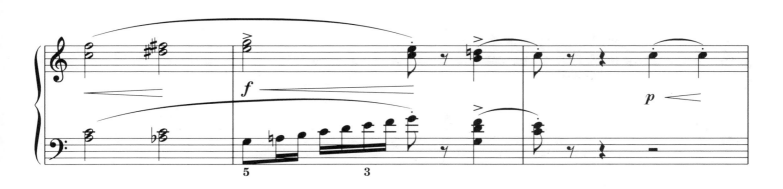

Johann Philipp Kirnberger
(April 24, 1721 – July 27, 1783)

Kirnberger was a pupil of Johann Sebastian Bach from 1739–41. He became a composer of many choral and clavier works, among which his fugues are outstanding. In 1751, he was violinist in the court of Frederick the Great in Berlin.

Lullaby

Johann Philipp Kirnberger

Peter Ilich Tchaikovsky
(May 7, 1840 – November 6, 1893)

Tchaikovsky studied composition with Anton Rubinstein at the St. Petersburg Conservatory. Tchaikovsky was a hard worker. Once when his teacher assigned him to write some variations, he stayed up all night and produced 200! All his life he worked for perfection and often destroyed the scores he wrote, thinking they were not good enough. In 1891, he visited America and conducted his own works at Carnegie Hall in New York City.

Russian Song
from "Album for the Young"

Peter I. Tchaikovsky
Op. 39, No.11

Carl Heinrich Carsten Reinecke
(June 23, 1824 – March 10, 1910)

Reinecke was court pianist for the King of Denmark for several years. He later became the Professor of Composition at the Conservatory of Music in Leipzig. Reinecke is best known as a composer, conductor, performer, and teacher. Cornelius Gurlitt was one of his pupils who later became a composer.

Prelude

Carl Reinecke, Op.183

Etude

Carl Reinecke

Ludwig van Beethoven
(December 1770 – 1827)

Beethoven deserves to be called the Shakespeare of music. He reached the heights and depths of human emotion as no other composer has done. Beethoven's ability to imagine melodies and harmonies, composing even when he became deaf, underscores his genius.

Ecossaise in G

Ludwig van Beethoven

Bagatelle

Ludwig van Beethoven

Ländler

Ludwig Van Beethoven

Franz Joseph Haydn
(March 31, 1732 — May 31, 1809)

Haydn was the first great master of the symphony and the string quartet. He looked on his genius as a gift from above and dictated the inscription on all his scores, large and small, "In nomine Domini" at the beginning and "Laus Deo" at the end. Mozart dedicated the well-known six quartets he composed to Haydn.

The Coffee Party

Joseph Haydn

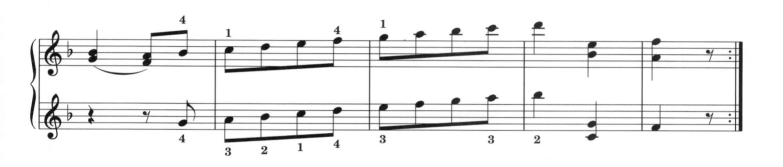

67

68

Contredanse

Joseph Haydn

Johann Friedrich Burgmüller
(1806 – February 13, 1874)

Johann Friedrich Burgmüller was a great German pianist and composer who wrote numerous piano works.

Arabesque

Johann Friedrich Burgmüller

The Limpid Stream
Op. 100, No. 7

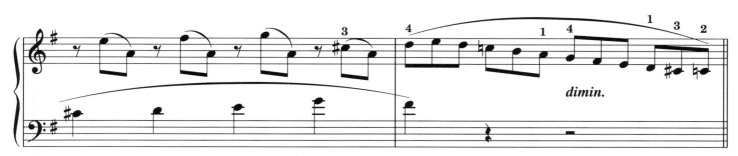

D.C. al Fine

Ballade

Allegro con brio

Johann Friedrich Burgmüller

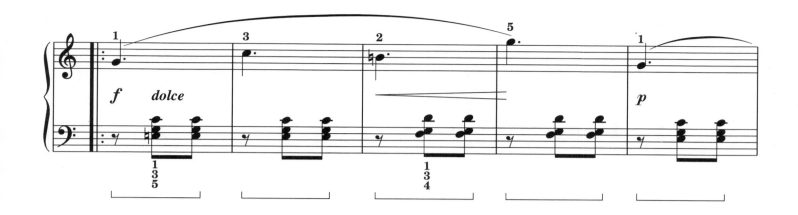

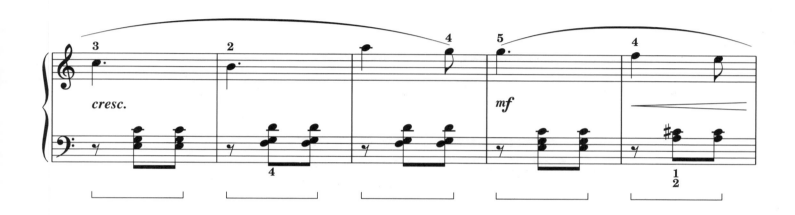

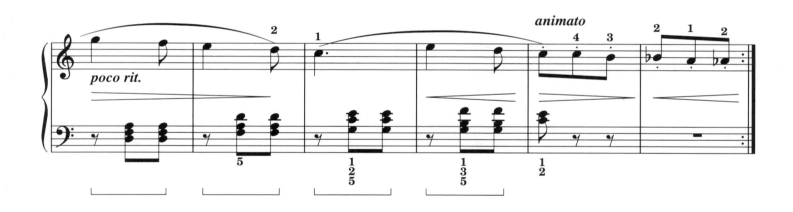

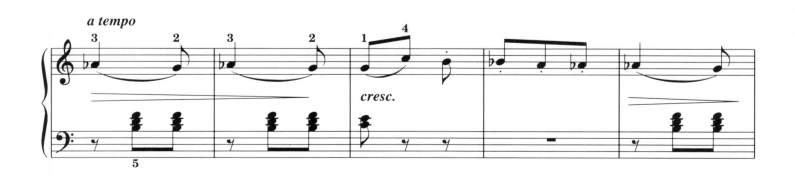

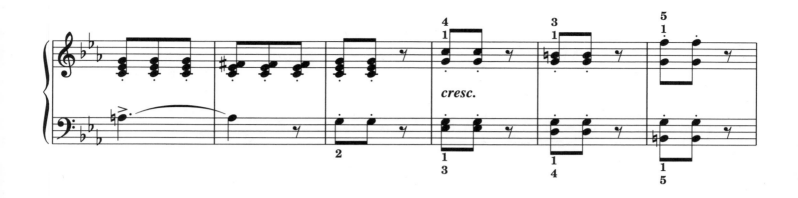

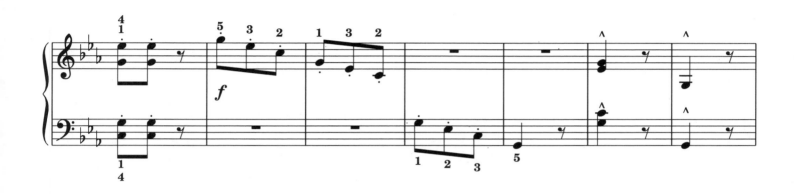

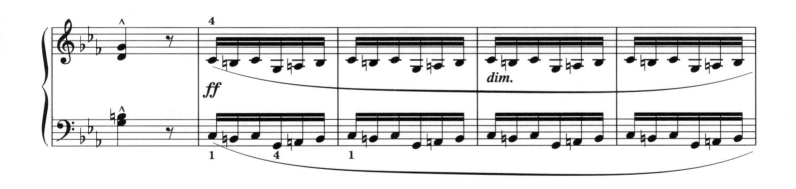

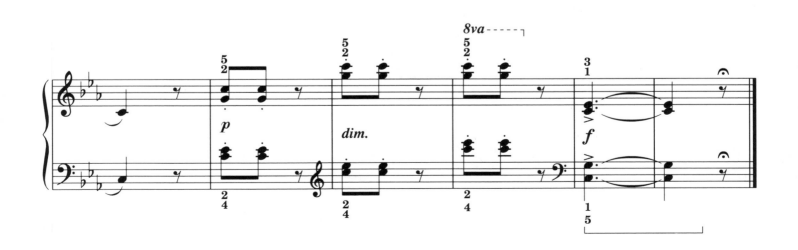

Progress
Op. 100, No. 6

Johann Friedrich Burgmüller

D.C. al Fine

James Hook
(June 3, 1746 – 1827)

This English organist and composer is said to have composed over 2,000 songs. He wrote a piano method, *Guida di musica*, in 1796.

Rondo

Andantino

James Hook

Henry Purcell
(c. 1659 – November 21, 1695)

Purcell was adopted by his uncle after his father died. He spent his childhood as a choir-boy of the Chapel Royal. When his voice changed, Purcell worked in Westminster Abbey as a music copyist and studied composition with John Blow. At the age of 20, Purcell succeeded Blow as organist of Westminster Abbey. Purcell married and had six children. He composed church anthems for cathedral services, numerous plays, and secular keyboard music. The Purcell Society was formed in 1876 to study, publish, and perform his works.

Old Dance Tune

Henry Purcell

Tempo di Minuet

Air

Henry Purcell

Prelude

Henry Purcell

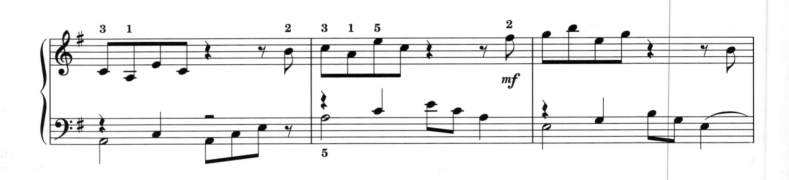

Trumpet Piece

Henry Purcell

Arcangelo Corelli
(February 17, 1653 – January 8/9, 1713)

This great violinist and Italian composer lived in the palace of Cardinal Pietro Ottoboni. He spent his life there composing and accumulating a rich collection of paintings.

Largo

Stephen Heller
(May 15, 1813 – January 14, 1888)

Heller was a popular pianist and composer who played in public when he was 9 years old. He became a friend of Liszt, Chopin, and Berlioz and was held in high esteem as a teacher and performer. He published a large number of piano works.

An Old Romance

Stephen Heller

Allegretto con moto (♩. = 100)

89

Christian Gottlob Neefe
(February 5, 1748 – January 26, 1798)

This celebrated German musician was Beethoven's teacher! Neefe composed many works, including piano sonatas and concertos for violin and piano.

Canzonet

Christian Gottlob Neefe

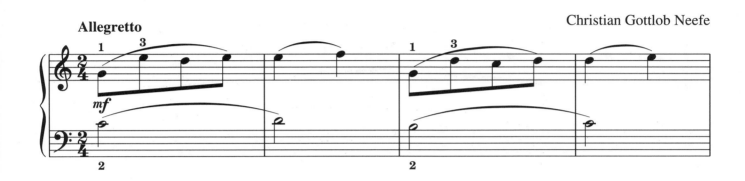

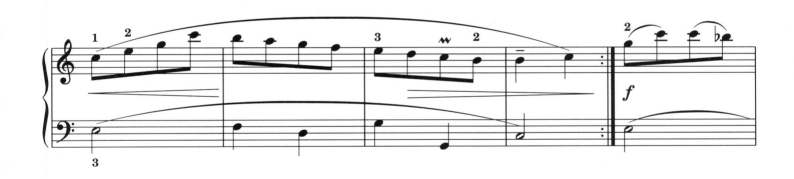

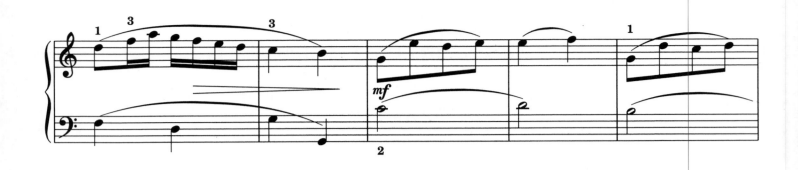

Johann Sebastian Bach
(March 21, 1685 – July 28, 1750)

The great Johann Sebastian Bach was born in German Eisenach. His brother became his teacher when his parents died when he was 10. Though so young, he longed each day for songs more difficult to play. These songs his brother did forbid and from Johann his music hid! But through the cupboard's latticed door Bach reached the tempting music score. And every moonlit night he wrote the precious copy note by note. Very secretly he learned and played, and then his brother was quite dismayed! But master of the fugue became, which won for him immortal fame. And though at last he lost his sight, his faith in God made darkness light.

Musette

Allegro giocoso

Johann Sebastian Bach

sempre stacc.

D.C. al Fine

94

Gigue in F Major

Johann Sebastian Bach

Minuet

from the Notebook for Anna Magdalena Bach

Johann Sebastian Bach

96

Preludio

Johann Sebastian Bach

George Frederic Handel
(February 23, 1685 – April 14, 1759)

Handel's father, a barber–surgeon, was 63 years old when his son George Frederic was born. Because his father wanted him to have a good education and not become a musician, young Handel would have to practice secretly in the attic.

Sarabande

George Frederic Handel

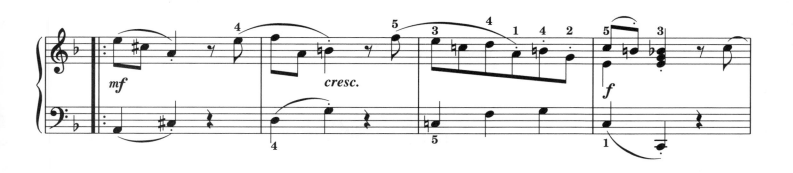

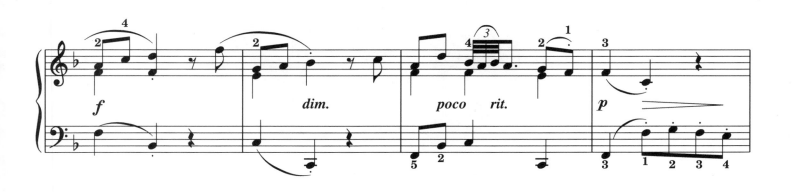

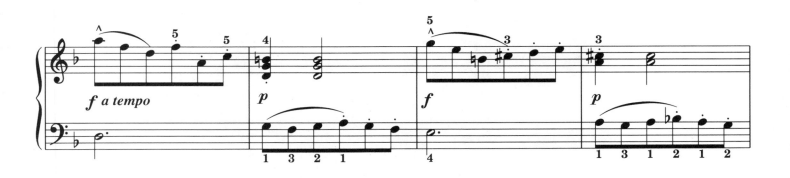

Carl Philipp Emanuel Bach
(March 8, 1714 – December 14, 1788)

Carl Philipp Emanuel Bach was the third son of Johann Sebastian Bach and became cembalist at the famous Court of Frederick the Great, serving until 1764, when the Seven Years' War put an end to the King's musical hobby. He then went to Hamburg, succeeding Telemann as director of church music there. C. P. E. Bach wrote 210 clavier pieces, including sonatas and 52 concertos with orchestral accompaniments.

La Caroline

Carl Philipp Emanuel Bach

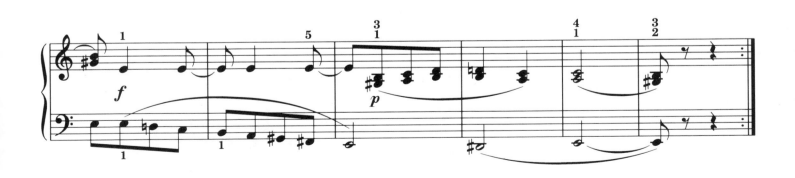

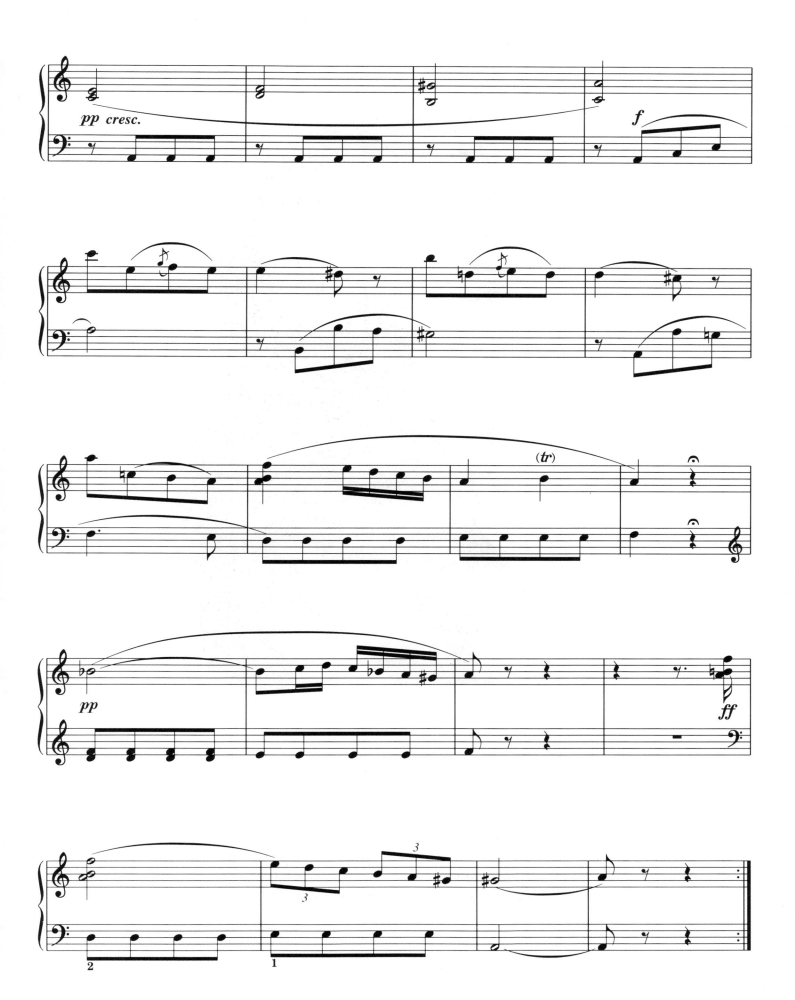

Wolfgang Amadeus Mozart
(January 27, 1756 – December 5, 1791)

Mozart and his older sister showed amazing musical talent at a very young age. Their father, Leopold, decided to commercialize their gifts and set up concert tours in many cities, including Munich, Vienna, Paris, and London. The concerts were very successful, and the children often played for royalty. Mozart began composing at age 5 and continued writing beautiful music all his life.

Minuet

W.A. Mozart KV 151

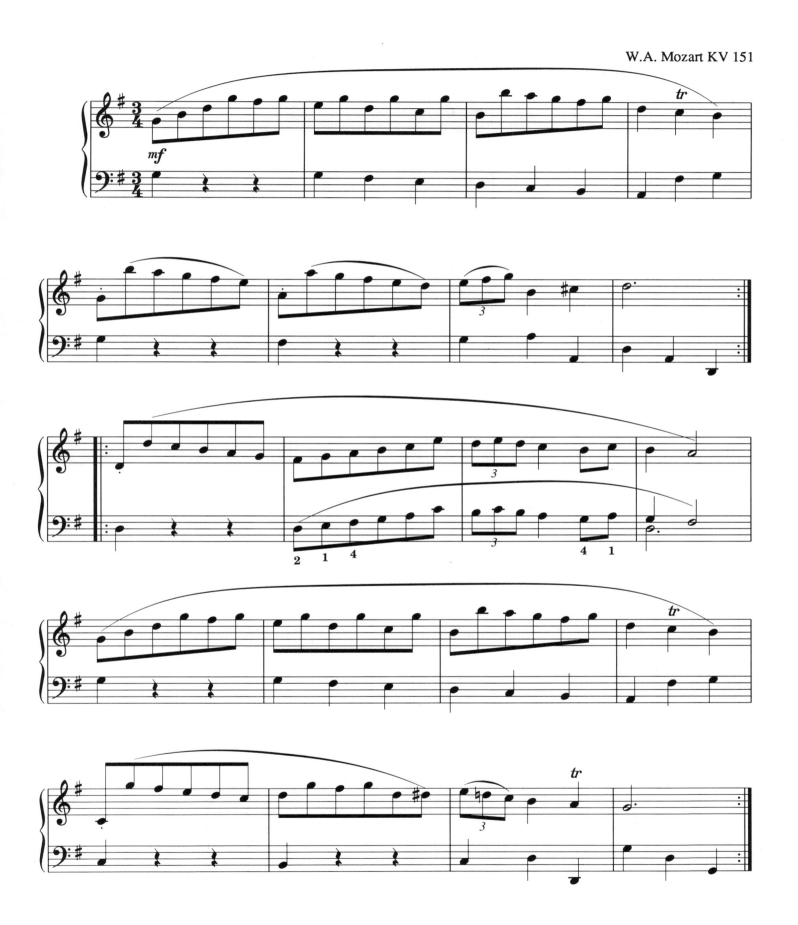

Minuet in F

W.A.Mozart

108

Minuet in G and Trio

W.A.Mozart

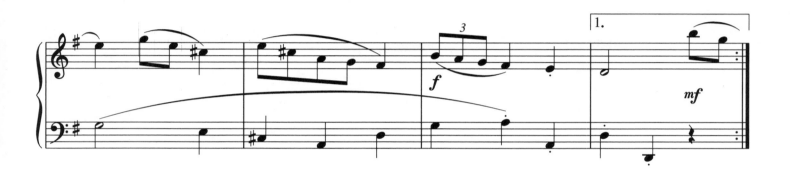

Fine

Men. D.C. al Fine

110

Leichte Klavierstücke

aus dem Londoner Skizzenbuch des achtjährigen Mozart

W.A. Mozart KV 1500

Menuett

Leichte Klavierstücke

W.A. Mozart KV 15e

Michael Ivanovitch Glinka
(June 1, 1804 – February 15, 1857)

This Russian composer is regarded as the founder of the Russian National School. He was the son of a wealthy land owner. He studied piano with John Field, but after only three lessons Field left and Glinka then studied with Zeuner and Mayer, becoming a very good pianist. He wrote numerous piano works, including five waltzes, seven mazurkas, and eight sets of variations.

Russian Polka

Hugo Reinhold
(March 3, 1854 – September 4, 1935)

Hugo Reinhold was a great pianist and composer who taught at the Vienna Conservatory. He wrote numerous piano pieces.

The Bagpipe

Hugo Reinhold
Op. 39, No.7

César Franck
(December 10, 1822 – November 8, 1890)

There was a dynasty of famous painters in his background, but young Franck was attracted to music. At the age of 11 he gave a concert tour through Belgium. In 1835 his father took him to Paris to study, and he entered the conservatory there. During an exam for sight-reading, he transposed the test piece a third lower without the slightest error or hesitation. This was not according to the rules, however, and Cherubini, who was the director of the Conservatoire, refused the prize to the young student, who was 15 years old at the time. Franck was awarded a special "Grand Prix d'Honneur." As an adult, his sole ambition was to be a composer. He composed every day, taught students, and was organist at the church of Sainte Clotilde.

The Doll's Lament

César Franck

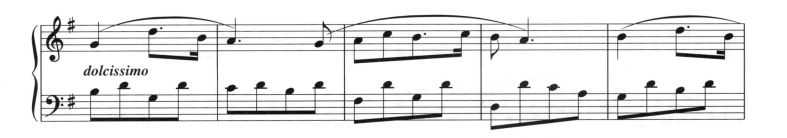

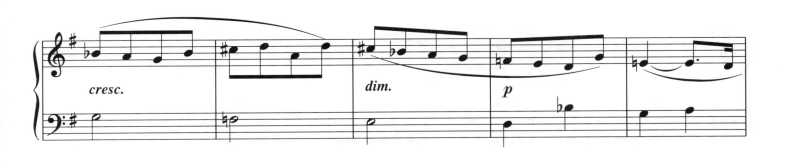

Muzio Clementi
(1752 – March 10, 1832)

Clementi's father sought out the choirmaster, Buroni, to teach his talented young son. When Clementi was just 14 he had written many works, including a Mass which caused quite a stir in Rome when it was first performed. He composed many sonatinas for the piano. Among his most famous pupils were John Field and John Cramer.

Sonatina

Muzio Clementi, Op 36 No.1

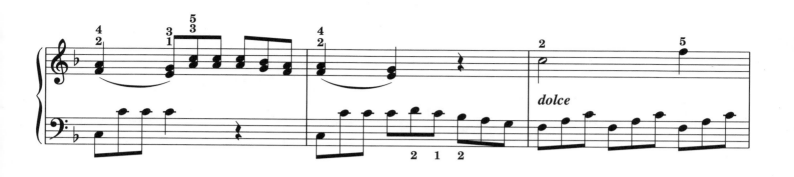

Rondo

Muzio Clementi, Op 36 No.1

Albert Elmenreich
(February 10, 1816 – May 30, 1905)

Besides composing many piano works and operas, Elmenreich was a German actor at the Court Theatre at Schwerin.

The Spinning Song

Albert Elmenreich

131